YOU CAN BE RIGHT . . .
OR,
YOU CAN BE HAPPILY MARRIED!

Maintaining Harmony In Your Christ-Centered home

Charlotte Volsch

CONTENTS

Foreword

The famous psychologist, Sigmund Freud, once posed a hypothetical question: *What is it, exactly, that women want?*

The answer turns out to be: the same as what all human beings want out of life: to be loved, to be fulfilled, and to find happiness, purpose and worth.

Charlotte Volsch has written an insightful account of her journey through life, from her upbringing in Indiana, to her single life in San Diego, her career, her marriage, and other significant trials she has faced along the way of maturing into a fully-realized and appreciated wife, mother, and servant of God.

Charlotte begins her story with how she dealt with being one of the middle children in a family of nine siblings, and her competitive and often failing attempts to gain her mother's and father's affections, and to forge her own identity. From her family experiences, and from keenly observing what went wrong and what went right in her parent's marriage, she embarks upon a new life in moving to San Diego, California, determined not to fall into the same traps that haunted her childhood.

Gradually, she realizes that her decisions to protect herself from being hurt and disappointed were not leading her to greater fulfillment, but rather having the opposite effect of putting her further down into a shell of isolation and fear.

Finally breaking out of this self-imposed prison, she finds her life opening up once again with her marriage to a man with similar views and goals in life.

However, after facing some of the many obstacles and trials that marriage entails, Charlotte finds that once again, old patterns assert themselves, undoing all her efforts to weave a tight marriage bond with her husband.

With the arrival late in life of her first and only child, Charlotte once again attempts to integrate what she has learned so far into dealing with the added pressures of motherhood, a career change for her husband, and economic setbacks.

What we find in these pages are a deep sifting through childhood memories and experiences, and an American woman trying desperately to tie all these threads together, using what the world's wisdom says should work for women, but often times, does not.

Charlotte makes the discovery that women sometimes sabotage their efforts to gain happiness, establish a solid marriage bond, and reap a rewarding motherhood by listening too much to how the world says they should behave. Only by keeping God at the center of their lives, are women able to keep everything balanced, to reach their goals, and to find what they originally set out to search for.

Ms. Volsch's brutally honest portrayal of her struggles to make sense out of what it means to be a modern-day woman, and her discovery that only a firm reliance on God can bring meaning, fulfillment, strength, and purpose in all areas of her life, makes *You Can Be Right . . . Or, You Can Be Happily Married!* a worthwhile read for every woman (and man) trying to understand why the *world's way* does not work, but *God's way,* does.

—Peter Marx, San Diego, CA
October, 1st, 2014

Chapter 1—The Awards Ceremony

I t was Saturday night at the awards ceremony for the year in reflection of Pitney Bowes Corporation.

I sat in the crowd and watched Andre's wife, as Mr. Bass read the list of accolades describing him: ethical, organized, deliberate, determined, results oriented, consistent . . .

Her expression was *dead pan*, an expressionless gaze—like that of a cold statue in a tomb.

When the room of five hundred and fifty people cheered, she remained expressionless, as I watched Andre rise and walk to the stage to receive his award. His walk was deliberate and determined, and he walked forward proudly, as the sound in the room of formal-attired guests rose. Many smiled and cheered. Some stood and clapped . . . but Andre's wife did not move.

I was puzzled by her very icy behavior, and wondered to myself why a person's spouse would choose, not only to downplay their own husband's achievement, but to deliberately damage their spouse's armor with such an obviously passive-aggressive chip on their shoulder!

It was then that Orv's name was called. I was so proud to see him honored, as I had worked with him for the past three years. At the announcement, Orv's wife broke into clapping with the biggest smile on her face. Orv, with his round, ruddy face and his big smile, almost skipped to the stage. He thanked his team, and mostly his wife, for supporting him throughout the year in his studies and travel, and announced that he could not have achieved all that he had without his wife's support, and knowing that she was always excited to see him come home.

Orv and his wife are not young newly-weds. They were in their late forties, with three children—two in high school, and one in college. But it was his wife who was his strength. You could see it, as Orv beamed when he spoke about her. She was his *Queen,* and it was evident in the way he respected her in her absence. Never once in the three years we worked together did I ever see Orv make any move towards another woman, or speak negatively about his wife.

This scene so resonated through my spirit. I *so* wanted to be that woman of strength, and not some stoic object. That mental snapshot allowed me to see the '*wind* beneath Orv's wings; the strength that fueled his spirit, the calm at the center of the turbulent waters of life.

I filed that scene away in my mind, and pull it out from time to time to see *how I was doing* in being the foundational support behind Cecil, my husband of seven years. How was I doing in encouraging him, with my full presence, my listening, my cheering, my stepping back to allow him to receive the accolades deserved!

The desire to be that kind of woman inside my marriage, *that* kind of woman of quality, had not always been there . . .

Chapter 2—Memories of Home

I was a middle child of ten children, raised in a very strict, organized, and often regimented household. We lived with discipline, boundaries, contribution, and commitment. But we also lived with a feeling of safety and security.

We were up at 5 AM to do farm chores: feed the pigs and cows, milk the cows, and then get ready to go to church at 6 AM with mom, a daily ritual and a vital source of regeneration for her, as I now reflect back upon those years. Like the proverbial postman—rain, sleet, snow, or ice, did not stop the ritual from being performed; and I remember my brothers getting out of the car on more than one dark winter morning, to push it out of a ditch where it had slid!

We went to service in the chapel of a Catholic nursing home, where my brothers assisted the priest during the service. The Sisters of Saint Francis ran the facility, and they often sent my Mom home with apples from their orchard, vegetables from their gardens, or eggs from their kitchen. I remember that there was a small vending machine at the top of the stairs, at the entrance of the waiting room, where we would wait before the service. All week we would save our nickels to use in the machine, and excitedly check to see what was available. *Snickers, 3 Musketeers*, and chocolate peppermint patties were the regulars.

After service, we rushed home. Mom would wake Dad up and begin to prepare a particular breakfast for him: specially-cut bacon, eggs over hard, special rye toast, and hot coffee (with lots of sugar). For us she would make scrambled eggs, white toast with bacon grease, and pour for us milk that had been collected the day before, from our own Lucinda, the cow.

My older sister was in charge of preparing each of our *brown bag* lunches, and my job would be to set the table with one of my brothers. When Dad came downstairs dressed for work, we would all gather around the table and give thanks: *"Bless us, O Lord, and these thy gifts, which we are about to receive, from Thy bounty, through Christ our Lord, Amen."* Then, after we all ate, Dad would rush off to the office in his suit and tie, and we would all grab our sack lunches and book bags and go stand outside, to wait for the school bus to pick us up.

After school, it was racing home, from the bus to the door, to see who could be first; then it was peanut butter and jelly sandwiches, homework, and if finished in time, a bit of playtime before dinner.

At 4 PM my Mom always took off her apron and went to *get ready* for Dad to come home. She always came out smelling like a bouquet of flowers and looking so *clean*!

At 5 PM Dad would be home, and we would all race out to meet him. He would immediately go inside to find Mom and give her his *greeting kiss*. We could hear them laugh and talk, as the kitchen window was usually open.

Dad would call us all in to wash for dinner, and we would pray the same as we had at breakfast time, and then all eat together.

My parents always showed kindness, respect, and affection for each other. Saturday was date night, when they would get dressed up, smelling very special, and go out to dinner and dancing. My mother loved dancing and looked forward to Saturday nights. My father always opened the door for her, helped her off and on with her coat, never used foul language, and never said an unkind word about her. My fondest memory of them is standing together on the front porch, with my dad's arms around my mom's waist, lovingly looking into her eyes.

The thought of this memory brings tears to my eyes when I realize what could have happened. From a child's perspective, one day it was safe and secure, and the next, it wasn't.

Things changed. My father reverted back to a behavior of drinking—no one but my mother knew—from thirty years before.

Maybe he had lost his dream, maybe life was at a point of struggle he could not muster through, maybe the combination of both of these, combined with drinking alcohol daily in his new position, pulled the rug out from beneath him. Nevertheless, he began to drink, and our lives changed— dramatically.

I remember when I was seventeen years-old, we were all ready for Christmas Eve service at 5 PM and waiting for Dad to come out of my parent's bedroom to join us, so that we could leave. When he came into the kitchen, my youngest sister ran up to greet him and he staggered and fell to the floor. At first, we thought he had tripped, and we all came over to help him; but from the look of horror on my mother's face, and her 'oh no,' it was evident that something else was wrong. He was not able to speak clearly as he answered her. I felt sick to my stomach. My mother ushered Dad back into their bedroom, and we then all left without him in a tense hush.

It was not going to be the same kind of Christmas that year!

A heavy feeling filled the car unlike past Christmas Eves when we sang Christmas carols on the way to and from church.

I could feel the strain in the air and almost dreaded Christmas Day, a day on which we usually laughed and shrieked with each gift opened. I knew this Christmas would be solemn, with a heavy *unknown* of what to expect. Mom had Dad admitted to the hospital, which was confusing to me because I did not understand alcoholic behavior. I had not experienced it before and I was not sure how serious his condition was.

After a week, he came home. I was told by my aunt he was in the hospital to *dry out*. My Mom never spoke of the Christmas Eve incident, but her behavior changed to cold curt replies to my Father when they spoke to one another. She became more absorbed in her art work, and Dad was no longer punctual. He did not leave for work at the same time everyday which often made me think, *Is he going to work today, or what?* Also, he did not appear as sharp or alert in the mornings, as he had before.

It became dangerous for Dad to take the car out at night. So, on more than one occasion, my sister and I disconnected the distributor of his car so that he could not start it. Inviting friends over became out of the question, because we never knew when he would walk out with a dazed look on his face, or begin slurring his words.

I felt like a young calf running through the woods, lost, and blinded by fear, running into trees. I felt like a *house of cards* that had a fan blowing on it, ready to tumble down.

Safety and security were nonexistent. Fear, insecurity, and shame took their place, instead. All the mortar began to crumble between the strong cement blocks of this thirty-year structure. Mom decided she that could not maintain her end of the marriage and run up this mountain again, by herself. She had based thirty years of her marriage on my Dad's commitment to her that he would not drink again, and this demonstration of broken trust and not keeping his word was more than she could handle.

I vehemently committed, right there and then, never to hold another person's word too tightly, not to marry, and not to have children—it was too painful.

That internal belief was confirmed as I began to date. What I experienced was a fear of letting anyone close enough to hurt me; and because of that, I chose relationships where I did not have to count much on the other person's integrity.

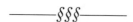

Michael lived three states away. We talked on the phone, wrote, visited one another three or four times a year, but neither one of us had any intention of moving, so it was a *safe* relationship for me.

Brian, another boy I dated, was from another country altogether. Going back to his homeland was always a possibility, which made another non-committed relationship, safe.

These boy-girl relationships were *fun for the moment* types of relationships, as long as they were not held too tightly. At least, on my part, I stayed cautious, kept distance between us, and expected no bonds or commitments.

At twenty-seven, the rudder of my ship began to turn, and the direction of my life did as well. The Bible says, "Train up a child in the way he should go; and when he is old, he will not turn from it."

I had moved out to California by this time, and my friends, Chris and Cathy, attended a non-denominational Sunday church gathering in the auditorium of an old school in Pacific Beach. It was not far from where they lived, which was in a small duplex near the beach. I lived in the valley but drove to meet them at their apartment, and together we would go to the service. After service, we would head back to their duplex and have breakfast, during which we would discuss what we had heard and experienced. Each week, as I took the time to experience the service, the message, and our discussions, I could feel a loosening to my belief that, insofar as relationships went, loose non-commitment was best for me. It was within the next two weeks that the message of *stop running* came to me through the Sunday service. I *knew* it was directed to me! I was beginning really look at my pattern of not having any long-term relationships with men, living with no real path forward in life—relationally, spiritually, educationally (even though I was working on my masters degree in business)—or making any of kind of contribution to anybody, or any thing.

I was not *getting hurt,* but I was not really *living*.

I took one big step of faith, standing in the kitchen of my apartment in San Diego. I remember saying, *"Lord I'm ready to stop . . . I'm ready to trust . . . I'm ready to let You guide me . . . I'm ready to give."* And with that came a new resolve to *try* a meaningful relationship with a man.

Two months later I met Cecil, and we have been married now for over thirty years.

Chapter 3—My San Diego Years

I was at *happy-hour* in San Diego with my girlfriends Chris (from church) and Wendy (from work). It was very crowded, so we shared two stools between us. Cecil was sitting on the next stool and struck up a conversation with Wendy, who is a very kind-spirited gal. After about thirty minutes, she turned to me and said, "It's your turn." My thought was, *No way do I have time for some barfly!* I was already in a *casual* dating experience. We began talking and he shared with me that he had just moved back to San Diego after having been gone for a year and a half. My heart softened at hearing this because I knew the lonely feeling of living somewhere that was unfamiliar. Because of this, I invited him to the small family restaurant that I managed up the road, for a cup of coffee *on me,* sometime.

About three weeks later, I was at *Houlihan's Happy-Hour* again with my *casual* dating partner, Bill, and saw Cecil. We exchanged *hi's* and I said, "Hey, I haven't seen you come by for that cup of coffee." He said, "No, but I will!" and away Bill and I went.

Several weeks later, as I was bustling through the restaurant during a very busy lunch hour, I caught a glimpse of Cecil sitting alone at a two-top, drinking a cup of coffee. I screeched to a halt and said, "Hey, great to see you!"

I picked up his check and told him, "As promised, this is on me. You'll have to come back again and let me buy lunch when it's not so busy."

I was pleased to be able to reach out and lend a warm *open door* to a stranger in town.

Cecil came by about two weeks later for lunch, after the *lunch rush* (12-1:30 PM is rush time). He asked what my roommate, Darlene, and I were doing that night, and I shared she was working at the *Hungry Hunter*, and that I was going by to see her for a bit, but then I had to study for a final paper I was working on.

Later, Cecil showed up at the *Hungry Hunter* and asked me to dance a couple of times while I was eating my nutritious, *happy-hour* gourmet dinner (free, in starving college days). I was true to my commitment to finish prepping for my finals, and he said he would call to ask me out on a "real date."

That first date, two weeks later, began a two-year committed relationship.

I must back up to say the *committed* part did not start immediately. It began with a month of casual dates—*casual* mostly on my part, because I was in a *casual* dating mode in my life.

About a month after the *first date*, upon dropping by my apartment unannounced to see me one evening, and finding out from my roommate that I was out with someone, he called later to see what was *up*. I told him that I had plans, and had not expected him to *drop by*. He inquired if I had a *boyfriend,* because he did not want to be intruding. I said that I did not have a committed relationship but only a few friends that I went out with from time to time.

"Oh," he said, "I would rather we had a relationship of just *you* dating *me,* only."

"Hmmmm," I replied, "Well, that could be possible but it will take some time for me to sever my other dating relationships."

"How long do you think that would take?" he asked.

I replied, "I would have to say, over the next two to three months."

My mind was thinking that that period of time would be enough to determine if this new relationship was going to be a *real* choice, while I slowly closed doors behind me . . .

Some relationship clicked closed quickly, while others squeaked slowly closed, and still others quickly slammed.

The steps along that path that allowed me to say *yes* were in the form of observations that I had made in Cecil's character: such as caring about his mom enough to visit her during holiday events, and making her a significant part of his life outside of the holiday visits, but not at a level of being unable to function without her. Another area I observed was his caring about his career enough to be concerned about his performance. Also, he was receptive and grateful for the time we spent together.

Months started going by, with life woven in. Oh, how I tested the durability of this relationship—with rudeness, obnoxious words, and (embarrassing now to relate), just very *not nice* actions, such as not even giving him a hug or a kiss good-bye when he was leaving for a two-day, out-of-town trip for work. This all happened before cell phones, you understand, so texting or calling did not take place in those spaces of absence. The *fear-filled* me was pushing him away. It was as if I were held hostage behind a stronghold, by a spirit force, a satanic spirit, a *non-me* force. This was a constant testing, to see if he would come back—exacting a punishment from him for not doing something I imagined he *should* do, without me asking, or him knowing.

As I sit here today writing this (thirty-one years later), a part of me wonders why he ever stayed with me. I felt he deserved someone who could appreciate him more for who he was, and yet I struggled with letting that part of me out, unable to allow myself any rejection, but instead to remain in a position of nonchalance if he ever might say that he was finished. Rejection was too painful; but if I pushed hard enough, and someone like Cecil left, it would be a *just as well* stance on my part, and would come as a relief, because closeness was much too scary.

Cecil always came back from his out-of-town trips with a forgiving spirit and a willingness to love me. I battled with the guilt of undeserved love. I was constantly looking for proof that it was *real*; that it was *true*. I would feel confident, and then I would receive a call from a close friend with the story of their divorce on the horizon, and that would rattle loose all my fears. What a roller coaster of emotion and uncertainty! I know now my *ungroundedness* gave rise to this high-rise teetering, without the earthquake-strapping feeling.

Had I first established a firm relationship with the Man who had given His life for me two thousand years ago, then the need or expectation from a human source would not have been so demanding, that it was incapable being met. As a boyfriend, Cecil was patient, as well as kind. He brought me flowers, gifts, gave of his time, lent his presence, and was able to mine the treasure lying beneath my rock quarry.

In February, 1982, I received a telephone call informing me that my dad had passed away from his short battle (short, because he had been diagnosed only that October) with cancer.

I had gone back to visit him in October, 1981 upon hearing of my dad's diagnosis. My brother, Bob, made it *easy* for me during that trip, by offering me a place to stay, transportation from the airport, and transportation to visit our dad. An older friend of mine had advised me to go, because they felt that if I did not go, I would only regret it later. Also, my friend helped pay for the trip; and to this day, I have a peace about putting forth the effort to make that journey. I have enormous gratitude to my brother and the friend who gave me financial, physical, and moral support, to allow me the opportunity to make the trip with ease and grace.

I was able to spend three hours with my dad alone—just the two of us talking.

I do not remember another time in my life of that ever happening, just him and me, since I was brought up in a large family of five brothers and four sisters.

Through his painful reflections about the sad dissolve of his marriage to my mother, I could finally understand that it was not a matter of him not spending time with me because of his rejection of me, but rather his grasping with the dissolution of this marriage brought about by poor choices that both he and my mother had made in life.

When I did get the call of my father dying, I was a newly-graduated but starving college student. It was the money question again as to whether I would be going to his funeral.

Cecil's encouragement spoke volumes to me. He did not have a close relationship with his own father, and he could have easily directed his advice to me from that place. I was most touched by his words, because in my heart of hearts I really wanted to go, and his encouragement to go, when he could easily have said, "Oh, it's OK; we'll just go do something to take your mind off of the situation," helped me keep the bigger picture in perspective.

Because my *love language* is in acts of service, his time investment in taking me to the airport, seeing me off, and then being there to pick me up on return, resonated very deeply with me.

In August, 1982, Cecil asked me to marry him. With that came a wave of anxiousness and uncertainty that would ebb and flow. The God I had consulted with, in my kitchen in San Diego the year before, was sitting on the side lines, waiting to be asked for help. I was too busy trying to figure everything out on my own to think that He might be of help to me. I was still thinking that I had only myself to depend on.

Pastor Joe, who came into the restaurant where I worked on Sunday nights after the evening service with his family, gave me some good questions to ask myself . . .

"Do you feel Cecil is a man of God?"

"Well, his dad was a pastor, so somewhere in there must be a connection. . ."

"Do you fully realize what the commitment of marriage is all about?

"I just want to know in advance that I would not have to experience the pain of rejection.

Wow, still all about me! I thought.

"What is at the center of your relationship?"

"Well, being happy right?"

So began a new journey for me—inviting God in from a reserved distance to be the orchestrator of my life, as He is today.

After discovering that Cecil had tax issues which needed to be resolved, I agreed to marry him on the day after tax day, April 16, 1983, on the condition that he had them all resolved.

Reflecting back with today's knowledge and experience is challenging, but it is where I need to go, to help that next person see the need for having a connectedness to the only relationship for life.

When nights were long, and a smile and flowers showed up . . .

When life was harried and coming home to find the house in order . . .

When I did another rude send off, only to get a message later, on the answer machine (remember those?), calling to let me know that I was missed . . .

When my Dad died, and Cecil insisted that I go to the funeral . . .

When we shopped for rings, because he wanted to propose and he said, "I can't afford what you deserve but I will pay it back on time."

When he cleared his taxes and his debts . . .

When he made a stand on addictions, and how he couldn't be associated with them . . .

We were married that day, April 16, 1983, and that was thirty years ago!

Working on what I wanted to be as a wife became a life-long journey.

Chapter 4—The Testing of a Marriage

Here we are, forty-five days before our thirtieth wedding anniversary and we have an opportunity to walk through fire—again; to again allow our emotions to come out and to be available to one another, to allow our selves to be kind, to love, to encourage, to refocus, and to be available.

I wish to relate my mental state during the traumatic circumstances of the scene I'm about to share with you. I was increasingly aware of finally being part of the marriage I had always dreamed of having. And this test came out of nowhere and became a defining representation of the two people we had become—allowing emotions to come out, being accessible to one another, allowing our inner selves to bent by kindness, to love, and to be loved, to encourage, to refocus, and to be available.

From the first words of "Charlotte, I just hit a guy and I think I killed him," a rush of adrenalin poured through my body and caused me to shake uncontrollably. At first, I had to sit down before I could stand. My mind flashed back to the call I had received five years before that began with, "I just did the stupidest thing in the world . . ." Then it leaped to little Brittany, who had died in my arms thirty-seven years ago after being hit by a car, which had pulled into the church parking lot and hit her, on Sunday morning. Next, my mind leaped to the voice of my high school friend running into the gym, where I was waiting for my sister to pick me up, shouting, "Charlotte! Come with us. Mary has been in an accident!"

I felt paralyzed and over-stimulated at the same time. "Call the appraiser and let her know I won't be there," he said, flatly.

I called Marilyn and I felt all quivery. I apologized for her driving forty miles for a meeting with my husband, but she just said, "Don't worry about that; we'll regroup at the end of the day."

It was now 10:30 AM, and I gathered my things together and put a note on the door explaining that 'I've stepped out; please call, and I'll be right over to show the model'. I got in my car and drove about a mile, but which seemed so much further. The backed-up traffic and emergency equipment alongside the road reminded me of my sister Mary's horrific accident on her way to pick me up from school, forty-five years ago. She had been badly injured and required two and one-half months of hospitalization. The other driver had been killed.

When I pulled over at the southern end of the blocked-off traffic on Apple Valley Road, I thought back to how I had had to run three-fourths of a mile from where my friends had parked to get to the scene of my sister's accident. Now, at this accident scene, I made the decision to go around to the northern blockade to get closer. As I pulled in to park in front of the apartment complex on the corner, I saw Cecil standing with D.J., our angel of mercy, who was also our insurance agent.

I walked over and put my arms around Cecil and he wept on my shoulder. I felt cold and sick at the pit of my stomach, as I looked over and saw the broken bicycle that the man had been riding, next to the bicycle path.

So much noise and commotion: people coming and going, reporters, fire department personnel, more police, detectives, everyone waiting for the D.A. to arrive.

Our son was at home packing for his weekly Christian mime group practice and Bible study. This particular Friday, he was going to a friend's house four hours earlier than usual, to work on a Bible study he was to be responsible for at next Saturday's workshop.

I gave Cecil another hug and said, "Remember, I love you," and he said, "Thanks for coming by to see me." I also thanked D.J. for staying with him and giving him counsel on what to do, and what not to do.

I felt I was in a surreal experience as I walked back to my car. I had to go and pick up Conrad to take him to Daniel's house to work on his studies. A woman called out to me 'Hello, Miss? Are you an attorney?' and I walked on, as if I didn't hear, and slowly drove off to pick up Conrad in a state of stupor.

My day was filled with appointments; fortunately, none with people I had to meet for the first time. Owen was my first appointment after dropping off Conrad, and he greeted me with his always enthusiastic spirit. I smiled and said, "Owen, I have something to share with you that has me a bit off track as I'm still trying to get my mind around it."

We went inside the escrow company and I told him that the road block on Apple Valley Road he encountered was because of an accident my husband was involved in, and although he had not been injured, the other man had died. Owen covered his head and cried out, "Oh no! Oh no!" I asked him to pray for the man's family, for comfort in their loss, and for Cecil's peace of mind.

Owen and his fiancé, Marie, had become *soul* friends in the four months that Cecil and I had worked with them in finding a new home and selling his current home. We completed his escrow paperwork together, hugged, and I sent him off to Los Angeles to meet Marie at the courthouse to get their marriage license.

My next appointment was at a property inspection for Gus and Maria. As I pulled up early to the property, I received a call from Penny who had seen my note on the door and was wondering when someone could meet her at the model. Cecil had called about an hour earlier to tell me that the police had taken his cell phone and iPad, so he was going to have to reactivate his *Droid* phone. I called *Verizon* to see if he was there, and Michael, the manager also a friend and client, said that he had left about forty-five minutes earlier, and that he had looked a bit shaken.

I reached Cecil on his cell and asked him if he was comfortable meeting Penny at the model, and he told me that he was. I called Penny, and she was delighted that he could meet her in twenty minutes. I was grateful that Cecil had some diversion from his thoughts.

The inspection on Gus and Maria's house, currently in escrow, went well.

Exhaustion was quickly taking hold of me as I drove to my last appointment with Candice to get a counter-offer signed. Candice worked nights and had just woken up from sleep, which allowed me to be equally subdued, as I floated into a surreal feeling, fueled by my own exhaustion.

Back home, Cecil looked exhausted. We hugged, and I felt his anguish. He had spent a considerable amount of time trying to get his new phone activated, meeting Penny, getting keys for key rings, all with his mind racing about the accident.

D.J. sent me a text mail, checking in on Cecil. Michael from *Verizon* sent me a text as well, letting us know he was praying for us. Owen also sent us a text mail, saying that he and Marie were praying, too.

It was now 8:30 PM—time to pick up Conrad from his practice and to tell him what had happened. I knew that when we pulled up to the garage and he saw the *Tahoe* missing, he would say, "Where's the *Tahoe*?" Sure enough, he did.

"I had an accident today," I heard my husband explain to my son. "What kind of an accident? What happened?" Conrad inquired. They followed each other into the house, as I went off to my room to change my clothes.

When I came back out I walked down the hallway to Conrad's room to pray with him before bed and to write in our *Gratitude Book,* as was our nightly ritual. His door was almost closed. I peeked in and saw him holding his head and rocking. My heart absolutely broke for the pain he was displaying. I walked away to leave him in his thoughts and came back about fifteen minutes later, when I heard him walk into the bathroom. His eyes were teary and he said, "Here's the *Gratitude Book*, Mom. You can take it and write in it. I just need to be alone awhile." He continued, "Most accidents are two cars and both have damage, maybe some cuts but pretty much OK, but Mom this is a biker, and he's dead." "Yes," I replied, "It is much heavier in our hearts for sure. Our pain all day has been immense." I hugged him a long time. Conrad and I both biked weekly and had an awareness of the alertness necessary when riding on busy streets and roads.

The next day was Saturday, and after his regular school review time with Cecil, Conrad said,

"Boy, Dad sure is different."

"How do you mean," I asked.

"Oh, he just seemed quieter today. I guess the experience of hitting the man on the bike yesterday was pretty big."

"No question. It is huge for him, son," I replied. "He needs your prayer for strength and comfort, as does the Olin family because they lost their dad."

A week has passed, and I have been at peace. I have finally finished searching through all the consequences of the accident: Department of Motor Vehicle information and reports, attorney articles, time and date for the funeral services, insurance reports and other matters. I have also listened to His still small voice: *"Rest in me, Charlotte. Be still, and know that I am God. Open your heart, and I will come and be by your side. I am here for you; I am your refuge."*

Only with His help am I able to be a wife in this process, allowing space for mistakes without reference to the incident. It doesn't need to define my husband. Being available, loving, and kind, and allowing for confidence to grow is sufficient. I check in with him at the end of the day, allowing space for him to be who he needs to be, with no *shoulds* to put on his shoulders. It also means not allowing his choices to impact what I choose to do— specifically, whether or not to go to Kevin's memorial service.

Walking through the door of *for better or worse*, brings you to *from better to best*, because there is a honing, a refining, a melding together that creates a closeness extraordinaire!

What an amazing morning I experienced yesterday, Saturday. Cecil and I had read together the night before (actually Cecil had read to me) from the book we were finishing and then we talked about our *tomorrow* schedules. I told him that I was going to the service for Kevin, and that I then had an appointment at 10:30 AM, at 1 PM, and at 5 PM.

"What time is the service?" Cecil asked.

"9 AM," I replied.

"And where is it?"

"At our Lady of the Desert, on Corwin Road," I answered.

He looked reflective and I left him in his thoughts, as he had mentioned on Monday that he did not feel comfortable going to the service, even though I had assured him then whatever he chose to do was okay with me, but I was happy to go with him if he would like.

As we walked back to the house from our reading time, Cecil shared his conversation with his friend Donnie from the day before. Donnie was to be at his sentencing hearing on Tuesday, as a result of something he had done. Cecil said, "I told him, 'you can't change what happened, or what will be the sentence; you can only change yourself as you move forward in life." He continued, "I told him many people care about you a lot." He told me he had also shared about God being available to help on this journey of repair, and that he was available for Donnie as a listening partner, too.

My insides screamed, "Wow, God, you are using him in such a special *out of self* way. Thank you!"

I told Cecil how comforting it must be to Donnie, who like him, has remorse and regret, and yet he chose to step out to comfort and encourage a friend. How amazing a friend is that!

Saturday morning Cecil was up early, as I. He came to tell me at 6 AM that he was going for a walk. He had a somber look about him. I gave him a hug and said, "Okay, enjoy the morning," and continued breakfast preparations and loading up the car. I lifted up my day to the Lord, asking for an open heart, and allowing Him to shine through, and then I proceeded to complete my morning dressing routine to become presentable to the world.

Cecil was back about 7:45 AM.

I asked, "Did you scale Bass Mountain?"

"No", he said quietly, "I just did the five mile route."

"Oh, that must have been invigorating," I replied, and then he went off to shower.

I took him his breakfast where he was showering and had a feeling in my soul that he was grasping the *going to the service* move in his spirit.

I came back to dress after I finished loading the car, and to kiss him good bye.

"Save me a seat," he said. "I'm coming, too."

My heart skipped for him. *Thank you, Jesus,* I said to myself. Never will he have to regret not going.

As I drove to the church, the roads were quite empty, which was not unusual for a Saturday morning. As I turned on Corwin Road towards the church, I was amazed to see very full parking lots, upper and lower levels, and all the way out into the dirt. *"Oh, my Lord,"* I thought, *"This man has touched many lives for You."*

I drove across the street to the *Century 21* parking lot, parked, and then called Cecil to let him know where to park, as the lot at the church was full.

"Okay," he said, "Thank you."

I walked up the hill to the church, and when I walked inside I was struck, not only by the fact that the church was full and chairs were set up along the back of the sanctuary room as well as a side room, but the somber yet peaceful spirit in the church.

I found an open chair against the wall in the back, with an open chair next to it, which I saved for Cecil. I kept watching both entrances for him as people kept arriving. I spotted him coming in by the same entrance I had used, and I caught his eye, so that he knew where I was sitting. He smiled and nodded as he stood in line to sign the guest book and then took the program and prayer card for Kevin's service.

I moved over so that he could have my seat, as the girl I moved next to was truly struggling with her loss, sobbing from moment to moment as she stared at the picture of Kevin that she held in her hand.

Cecil sat next to me, and I could feel and hear his quivering breathing, as he reached for my hand, and I squeezed his hand back.

The service was beautiful—in song, in readings from the Word, and in reflection on Kevin's giving heart for others, and for the Lord. Prayers were said for his family, for the church, and for the driver (I smiled inside and said, "Thank you").

Cecil continued to reach out for me, and we sat and stood, arm-in-arm, through each segment of the service.

As the communion segment began, he told me that it was 10:05 AM. He asked me if I thought that he should leave since he was supposed to open the office at 10 AM. I told him that whatever he was comfortable with was fine with me, but that I had to leave in 10 minutes to meet a client at 10:30. A few others were beginning to leave and we left at 10:15.

As we walked out and started down the hill to where we had parked, Cecil said with tears in his voice,

"I'm really glad I went."

I squeezed his hand and said, "Yes, you will never regret that you didn't."

A few more steps and he said tearfully, "Wow, he was a really great guy."

"Yes, he was," I said. And then I said, "You're a really great guy, too, my love, and God chose you to help bring him home to Him and wants to hone you through this experience to do even more for Him in the time you are here."

He continued to walk with me as the tears continued to roll down his cheeks in the morning sun.

Marriage is a journey . . .

It is a journey of many difficult steps and twists and turns.

It is one of the hardest journeys of the 'whole life' journey because it's not about 'you' . . .

It's not about 'we' . . .

It's about 'HIM'!!

I truly believe the most difficult part of the journey is realizing just that . . .

It's about HIM . . .

And with that realization comes a new outlook on what I do or don't do; how I do what I do, and the realization of the consequences for what I do, and then owning up to them.

It is about having a servant's heart and a giving spirit. It is about believing in another more when they are down, then they believe in themselves, and until they believe in themselves more fully. It is about giving more of what you want. It is about being available when you want to be alone. It is about being kind, compassionate, and grace giving . . .

Marriage is God ordained, and by going to Him daily to bless, guide, and strengthen my walk with Him and my actions around me, then and only then, do the fibers of the cord that bind our marriage together grow stronger and become knit more tightly.

Chapter 5—Not Taking Charge, Fostering Harmony

O ver the years I had worked on and developed leadership skills through higher education, the school of hard knocks, and through career training. The shift to "neutral," after being in the leadership 'gear,' is a thought-filled shift. It requires a *pattern interrupt*, so to speak, to accomplish the shift, because the busy life of constantly searching for what needs to be done next must halt. Not that all *doing* must come to a screeching halt, but that a thoughtful look at *what* is being done takes place, to see if a different action would be more suitable for the intended results.

Here is one of many examples I can share with you, where I first learned and began to develop my own insight into this process.

When Conrad was a new-born and things were changing dramatically in Cecil's career regarding territory and income, I thought I had a solution. I would help Cecil out by also working in his territory with him, since I knew the business and my participation would add to his efforts, and ultimately, to our income.

After to choosing to end my career at a Fortune 250 company in a high level management position in order to begin a new chapter of *family*, Cecil received a new territory assignment within the same company, which required him to make a great number of business-to-business calls to *very* small businesses, in order to explain to them the benefits of upgrading their systems, and to share with them the newest technological updates.

Because I had worked for the same company and knew the products, the approach to businesses and the presentation, I thought it would be beneficial for me to make calls on at least five businesses a day, which would help Cecil reach his quota of twenty calls per week.

I was delusional and feeling self-congratulatory. And then one night, as he was discussing his day and his upcoming review, I mentioned how relieved and excited he must be to be able to have the *cold call* quota met. Cecil thanked me for my help but seemed less than enthusiastic. I looked up from draining the chicken I was soaking in marinade for the grill and asked,

"Do you have some concerns about your meeting?"

"You know Charlotte, I really appreciate your help, but I feel as though I'm failing at *doing my job.*"

"Hmmm," I said, "Why do feel like that?"

"I just feel like you are better at doing the calling, because you have more success at it than me. You're better at organizing and following through with making the calls every day and week, and I just feel like I'm failing at fulfilling my commitment to my family in supporting them."

I was stunned that my efforts I was so proud of contributing were more destructive than enhancing.

I walked to the grill to cook dinner in a stupor and thought through my actions and made a mental note that, *When I take charge things get done, but at what price?*

> *Lost learned lessons by him.*

> *Guilt he has because of me having to do more.*

> *Weakening of his strength.*

> *Resentment on my part of having to do more.*

> *A growing wedge.*

Two years later, Cecil decided to pursue a new career of real estate. I was a new, stay-at-home mom and wanted to support his efforts, but in such a way that would be supportive and encouraging.

I chose to prepare him for each day with presentation binders for his appointments, support documents for transactions, and scheduling appointments for him throughout the day. I helped by listening to his practice presentations, and encouraging him in his skills development. On more than one occasion, Cecil said to me, "I so appreciate your help! You make my job so much easier with all that you do."

What I learned from all this was that responding to *asks for help* are much different from *taking charge*. One difference is that *asks for help* are all about being willing to cooperate with another's request, while *taking charge* is all about telling someone what to do, or what not do, with words or actions that create a *not good enough* atmosphere, instead of a *I'm proud of you* atmosphere.

I also learned that it is difficult to be *proud* of someone, when *I'm* doing what *they* should be doing. Additionally, I learned that it is impossible for my husband to feel respected, when *I'm* doing what he feels *he* should be doing.

The end result? A lot of *should-ing* ends up going on, and separation and distance being created, instead of closeness and *shared-ness,* and ultimately leading to both of us just *existing,* instead of *bonding.*

So, here are my thoughts for you: has it happened in your life, possibly, that you may have had a boss, or a parent, a coach, or a mentor, who succeeded in motivating you to reach your *peak* performance, and allowed you to feel that anything was possible? Ask yourself: what was it that this person did, to give you that feeling of, *I've got this, I'm appreciated, I'm accomplishing something, and they are proud of me?*

For the next five minutes, write down who that person in your life was (or maybe still is), what was it that they did, what feeling did their *doing* elicit inside of you, and what lessons did you learn about yourself, as a result of your *doing* that they encouraged.

Now, think back to your role as a wife and partner: have you ever tried to *take charge,* instead of *helping out?* Maybe, you did it quite reflexively, so that you did not realize you were doing it at the time.

Think about what was the *big picture accomplishment* that you had in mind, which motivated you to take the action that you took. For me, in the example I gave of calling on business customers, it was in helping my husband reach his quota more easily, and to not feel pressure from his boss for not making the calls he disliked the most.

Then, recall what was the result of the action you took, and what affect it had on:

The big picture goal

You as a wife

You as a mother

Your husband, as displayed in his words, body language, humor, self- mocking tone, etc.

Now, in retrospect, with the advantage of this piece of perspective, what could you have done differently to allow your husband to feel his own strength and success, and where you could have fostered the feeling of strength and harmony?

It is in our husbands' *DNA* to be heroes. If we are rushing to *save the day,* it defeats their chance to be our champion.

Over time, I've learned to hold back and to swim beside my husband, coming in as requested, like a synchronized swimmer, where amazing progress towards a goal is made gracefully and in unity.

In my world, I have witnessed and experienced the feedback from this different approach to *helping out,* and also of having it confirmed from others looking at the unity that Cecil and I have together.

Learning a new skill is the easy part. Putting it into practice in an ongoing fashion is the challenge. What I have done and continue to do, to stay on track, or to do a course correction, is three-fold:

Daily reading of the Word, and seeking HIS purpose and guidance in my life and role as a wife. Taking that morning quiet time to reflect and connect, allows me to hear the still, small voice, and to see where I need to ask forgiveness, or to change my course, and then to take the action necessary, whether it is in the writing a note, sending a text, making a phone call, or giving a big hug!

Having a prayer partner to keep me accountable to my biblical role as a wife, which, if followed, allows my husband to fulfill his role, as husband.

Having a life coach that pushes me to my peak performance in all aspects of my life, which keeps me from going into my husband's life, to find things to 'take charge' of.

Chapter 6—Unity: Supporting a Common Cause

s a family, what is your cause?
What do you want your life to represent . . . together?
Unity is strands woven together, like a chord of rope.

It is strength in relationships, creating strength in families.

The strength is doubled and tripled because of the weave, allowing more stress, more weight, more endurance.

Unity is NOT competition, and because of that it requires a total gear shift from the competitive work environment to a synchronized, dual force.

From a "how am I going to strategize a 'win' to 'how am I going to pull together."

From a pushing, to a pulling . . . again, like the strands coming together in an integrated weave.

In our first fourteen years of marriage, Cecil and I were immersed in our careers, not to the exclusion of each other, yet allowing it to consume a significant part of ourselves.

Cecil began allowing me a little more intimately into his career life when his boss asked me to come to work for him, after I had mentioned to him that I was looking for a job that allowed Cecil and me more time together than what my restaurant owner/manager position allowed.

I told Cecil's boss, Pat, that I would have to talk it over with Cecil, because our relationship was more important to me than a job working with him. Pat honored that and said that if it was all right with Cecil, then it was all right with him. This began the chapter of having separate careers but inside the same company.

We supported each other in our monthly work efforts to exceed quota goals and strategizing training segments when we were in team leadership positions.

We invested time in our marriage relationship by setting aside time daily to talk, and to be together on weekends, to recharge and refresh, either at the river, or in strategizing at the office, or in preparing for a trip necessitated by our jobs, usually to either Connecticut or San Francisco.

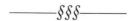

In 1997, Cecil and I had a son—Conrad. This was a monumental experience for us for many reasons.

Because of the pain of my parents divorce, and the experience of some of my siblings turning against either one, or both, my parents, I decided that I never wanted to:

1.) raise children as a single mom

2.) go through the horrific rejection I had watched my parents experience.

Also weaving into that mix of past memories, was the fact that one of my ovaries was not working properly; so I imagined I was not capable of giving birth to children.

It was Christmas Day 1996, and Cecil and I were celebrating Christmas together ourselves, since it came in the middle of the week. We were happy about that because it would be fun and quiet and just us, with Christmas music, his favorite pot roast, and a fire glowing in the fireplace.

At work, Cecil was moving to a new office beginning January 1st. He asked if I minded that he went to work on it that morning because no one else would be there, and he could get so much more accomplished with no interruptions.

I felt unusually weary but said, "Great idea. Go knock it out, and I'll have a great dinner waiting when you get back, late afternoon."

"OK", he said, "I'll call before I leave, to see if you need anything."

"Perfect," I said, and off he went.

We had gone to Christmas Eve service the night before and had experienced a breathtaking service, with lights, candles, singing, the orchestra, and the celebration of Christ's birth. I was so tired before we went, that Cecil walked across the street to buy me a cup of coffee, as we waited in the long line to be seated.

So here it was, Christmas morning, as Cecil told me about going to the office, and I was feeling as if I had not slept, and yet I had. I looked forward to taking a Christmas nap while he was gone.

When I woke to prepare dinner, I still felt tired and now, in addition, I felt slightly nauseous. Please bear in mind that my husband and I had been childless for over thirteen years, yet a still small voice whispered to me and said, *Get a pregnancy test,* to which I replied, *No way; I'm now forty-four years old. This just can't be!* But then, as I said, anything is possible through Christ.

Cecil came home to the feast I was preparing, and in the middle of dinner he remarked, "I'm so sorry I didn't call you before I left, to see if you needed anything."

"Just as well," I said. "I think you might have fainted if I had told you what I really needed."

"What do you mean?" he replied.

"I was going to ask you to get a pregnancy test kit, and I was glad that you didn't call, because I wanted to ask you in person."

Cecil was so excited. He hugged me, kissed me, and then ran out to find an open drug store. He came back with a kit having two testers . . . just in case!

The first test came back *positive*, and I felt a surge of fear and anxiety roll over me, like I had never experienced before. I waited a few hours and tested again and received a second, confirming *positive*. Now, Cecil was flying high with elation, and we began a jumbled conversation as to what we should be doing differently now, to bring up this little person.

We decided that having one of us home would be critical, along with homeschooling. I also decided that I would need to increase my daily walking to prepare my body for the event. We decided to read up together on what to do, how to do, and when to do. So many thoughts and ideas began fluttering around, as we began to weave our unity around the expectation of being parents, with a tight foundational cross-weave and braid. Our goal was to be intentional about being good parents, rather than just accidental parents.

I was so proud of Cecil as he took on the role of being the sole wage earner, after thirteen years of being a family with two incomes.

Conrad was born the following August. So much to be grateful for—he was healthy, I was healthy, and a new chapter in my life began, of being both a wife, and a mother.

And, I was excited and happy to have the opportunity to take on both roles. Throughout our fourteen years of marriage, I did feel that I had been a good wife to my husband; but now, I could truly pour myself into serving as a helper to Cecil in the way he deserved. Daily, I made breakfast, packed his lunch, had dinner ready at the end of the day, put notes in his lunch bag and on his mirror where he shaved, all because he was my focus, along with baby Conrad. No longer was I consumed with attending corporate meetings or putting out client fires. I found it a joy to set out Cecil's clothes for him to wear, to go outside with the baby to waive goodbye every morning, and to welcome him home each evening. I loved doing his laundry, and ironing his shirts, and seeing them all hung like little soldiers in his closet.

After the first year, our unity was met with Satanic attacks. There were major changes at Cecil's workplace territory, from cuts which reduced his income by 50%, to pension plan reductions of over 75%.

Cecil began searching for alternative sources of income and found an opportunity working at the airport for *United Parcel Service*, cleaning their cargo planes at night from 10 PM to 3 AM, or from 11 PM to 6 AM, four nights a week. He and a partner would wait in the cleaning truck near the parking area where the planes came in and nap, while waiting for the next plane to arrive, clean that plane, and go back to napping and waiting. He would come home between 6 and 7 AM, read to Conrad, shower, take a nap, and then work his corporate job. About a month later, he found an opportunity to learn the lending business, in a brokerage office that processed a lot of loans. He worked the phones, took calls, processed applications, and initiated the qualifying process. For the next four months, he worked from 10 AM to 4 PM in his sales position, 4 PM to 9 PM learning the lending business, and then three to four nights cleaning planes, from either 10 PM to 3 AM, from 11 PM to 5 AM.

I had applied for, and interviewed for work at Denny's, (the 11 PM to 6 AM, or 10 PM to 6 AM shifts) but they thought I was over qualified. I realized that pouring myself into Cecil's efforts in supporting us was now my most important investment of time. l still had everything ready for him as before, as well his change of clothes. Sometimes, I would meet him somewhere, to bring him food and clothes; at other times, I would have everything ready for him when he arrived home for a quick nap and change.

I was so proud of his courage and commitment to do whatever was necessary to support his family. In addition, the Lord blessed him with great health in this trying chapter of his life, fighting against Satanic attacks, and our chords of unity were woven even more tightly and more deeply together.

After the four months, he was able to let go of a twenty-two year career with a *Fortune 500* company, which allowed him to reach out and grab with both hands his new position of helping people qualify for, and to buy a home. He poured himself into learning everything possible about the industry, the market, the rules, and the guidelines.

As the size of his business grew, I began taking online courses to lend him support, by getting my real estate license.

Having a license was a requirement in the real estate industry to do many of the things with which he needed help.

I was able to set aside some time to set up appointments for him, or to prepare documents during Conrad's nap times and play times, as we wove and knit our chords even tighter together. And we pulled together again in whittling away at the debt that had accumulated from the change in our income, and the reinvestment of income into a new industry.

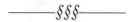

Like many women, the realities of life required me to be occupied full time in the workplace while Conrad was in the fourth grade. I took on responsibility of learning markets, memorizing rules, following guidelines, and completing paperwork in a very compressed period of time, and the tightness of our weave suddenly began to unravel. I felt overwhelmed with the huge requirement of being skilled, knowledgeable, and maintaining dependable performance. Because of that, a loss of teaching and review time with my son occurred. In addition, I had no time remaining to prepare meals for Cecil anymore, or to lay out clothes for him, which left me feeling a sense of incompleteness—feeling sucked dry, like an empty juice box. I could literally feel the unraveling of our unified cord of strength my husband and l had committed to weave, together.

Because of the need for us to achieve financial success quickly, I felt angst and double pressure which pushed both of us to the level of excluding one another. In other words, my husband and I were no longer working together on his accounts, or even our own business plan. The result of this was that he began to lose confidence, and my time requirement "in the business" was growing more and more, with less of me left to invest into our home and into our son's education—our original commitment to one another. The joy that I had received from investing myself into that important part of our lives was being pushed aside for another routine I had once loved as a career, but now no longer had any desire for. I was frustrated that it could not all just *work out,* and I was resentful of the extra time I was required to give, but just did not have. There was no pulling together any longer; the tight weave was beginning to unravel; and as I scrambled to slow it down, to put a knot in it the minute before re-braiding the weave, I was asked to reunite, reunify, rewrite our game plan, for making all the parts work effectively.

There was a *yo-yo* inside of me, one side wanting to reinvest in that unity of strength that was our home, the unified force behind our efforts to reach results, and just wanting to stop!

Stop "trying"

Stop "giving" more of me, more time

Stop "doing" for everyone

To What . . .

With one you can go fast . . .

With two you can go far . . . and weave an unparalleled strength.

I hated, but also loved, the fact that the still, small voice could still be heard. It was comforting to be reminded of the true strength in life, but also an awakening for me to answer some tough questions:

Whose way was I following?
Had I taken time to invite in my Lord on this pushing apart?
What was His purpose for my life?
What was His purpose for us in this segment of our journey?

Together we made the choice to restructure, to strengthen for unified endurance, and to re-braid the weave in order to bring strength beyond repair, and now walking with HIM, as the third strand in our braided weave. When I could honestly say to myself that I wanted to live with HIS purpose filled life, I became open to seeing the steps necessary to rebuild our unity, beginning with an r e n e w e d agreement of *together in everything,* in all of our life. The biggest tools in my tool belt were now, G*race* and *Forgiveness.* I borrowed them from Christ, because He was using them on me.

Something to think about—

Think of a team you were part of that just clicked . . ..

What was your position on the team? What was your con-tribution to the team?

What in your opinion made it 'click'?

What I've discovered is that unity requires a unique vulner-ability, which is a willingness to be humble enough to say I goofed, I don't have all the answers, I got off track from building together, to running on my own. It is a willingness to first forgive myself for running off course, and second, to forgive my husband for doing whatever I think should have been done differently. It is a decision to begin reweaving the chords. The amazing discovery is that the strengthening in the weave surpasses the strength that was there before!

Lesson

- Make a list of your current concerns or unmet needs . . .

- What would you like your husband to do differently?

- What would you like him to change to better meet your needs?

- Now make a list of what your husband may say his unmet needs are . . .

- What might he say he'd like changed to better meet his needs?

Chapter 7—Know Thyself: Refill, Recharge, Re-energize

Much giving is required in life as a woman . . .

Giving life

Giving love

Giving encouragement

Giving foundation

Giving education

Giving nourishment

Giving care

L ike the juice box, if you aren't refilled, the contents are drained dry; the container rings empty . . . the giver stops giving . . .

Let me say it again—the giver stops giving.

Without refilling the box with juice, the heart with love, the mind with a connection to Christ, the body with rest, there is a slow and progressive emptying, disconnect, and death.

So what is it that awakens:

Your heart

Your spirit

Your physical self

What is it that drives your passion to give?

I can share depletion because that is a state I have experienced recently on many levels:

Requirements for our son's education

Requirements for my licensing due

8 files at the top of processing

Pains shooting through my body, some with unknown sources

Exhaustion throwing me down

And then I was rescued by a message through my pastor... "slow down," "say no," "wick down the drive," "know where *drive* is taking you."

More isn't necessarily better. The quality of what is given is most important.

To be a source of light, the candle must be steady and the wick trimmed.

To be a source of life, the river must be filled and the debris swept away.

Learn to say 'no' to the good, to say, 'yes,' to the best.

For me, I hit the reset button daily, beginning the first thing each morning. I call it my morning ritual, and I learned how to make it *ritual* from my business and life coach and friend, Joe Stumpf.

Although I loved being up before everyone else in my household, in order to experience quiet peacefulness, when I learned how to invest that time in a ritual, the dividends which rewarded me were priceless. It was clearly evident in physical, spiritual, and emotional payouts, which have allowed the giving to flow, and not to feel like a *duty*.

I am up at 4 AM and begin my first steps with either speaking, or reading, a verse or phrase that allows my first hearing and listening of the day to be positive and purposeful.

For example:

"Thank you for this day, Lord, as I look to You and live it in such a way as to be a light for You." Or, "I'm grateful for this day to live a life on purpose, with You working within me." Or perhaps I read something from the Book of Psalms.

I read from the book I'm currently in with my reading partner, or I read from the Bible in conjunction with my weekly Bible study, or perhaps the book from my weekly Book Readers Club, which centers around business or personal development.

I write with inspirational purpose, in order to send out a daily inspiration to forty-eight others, each morning.

I do a work out routine of stretches, crunches, weights, and sometimes, a bike ride.

All of this is completed in a two-hour time frame, and then it is on to breakfast preparation, with a relaxed and inspired face on my day.

In fact, it is through this morning ritual that I began to have the seed watered for writing this book in 2009. In 2011, it was fertilized with Joe's coaching, and in September, the journey began.

Writing has been a gift to me, which has allowed me a medium through which I can express myself without judgment. I have been able to say what is on my heart, to flush out toxins, and to plant the seeds of future crops, by expressing my creative self, often times in seeing events from multiple perspectives.

My *me time* allows me to feed this passion, which in turn fuels the growth of my *best me* and my *servant heart*, both of which give me inner peace.

The physical development focus of my morning routine allows the toxins of my body to be squeezed out, much like the toxins of my mind are flushed out.

The results of this ritual are:

A day begun with a renewed perspective.

A refilled juice box

Love in my heart to give

It is the quiet time that allows the *Voice* to be heard of *what is*, which is the source of all recharging, refilling, and re-energizing. It all comes full circle, beginning with my time with God, first! Short-changing that time blocks all other efforts. Neglecting that connection, for me, invites disaster in the race course ahead, and visibility in the present remains cloudy.

I am so grateful that He sees my usefulness to Him, because with that I get *taps on the shoulder,* to wake up and change course before a crash is experienced, and to teach what I have learned, so that others can benefit and grow.

I can best hear His voice in the quiet time of morning, or on my bike rides, with the wind blowing in my face, breaking a rushing smile across my face, as I drink in all of His creation; or on the hiking trail, as I marvel at the voices of nature, and the change of view with each turn; or in my gazing out across the water at the lake, the ocean, or even listening to a river ripple, or the stillness, or the crickets, or the birds.

Getting up and getting going, day after day after day, almost gives a continued feeling of always being able to do just that . . . until the props are knocked out from under, but little conscious thought is given to this process.

With my daily morning ritual, I no longer feel torn between caring for myself, and caring for my family. In fact, I have come to the realization that not caring for myself is truly not caring for my family. It is not an either/or, but instead a part of the complete formula and a big piece of the weave of unity. It is the only way to be the best wife, the best mom, the best executive, the best entrepreneur, and the best encourager and super-servant.

For me, finding reasons to steal from this critical self-refueling time is a no-win proposition.

Making God the first step in each day is to stay in touch with the true source of energy, allowing me to see the stumbling blocks in my way, and to stay in touch with the spirit within me, and being able to draw upon His wisdom.

This is my *secret sauce*.

Consider these things: 1) self care is critical. It is like when the flight attendant instructs you to put on your oxygen mask first before helping anyone else because your efforts are less effective when you don't fuel yourself first.

2) if you just received a call that guests were coming in tomorrow morning and could stop by for 30-45 minutes what is one thing you would want to do for them in that 30-45 minutes to let them know how special they are? This is the same level of stop and do mindset you need to have daily. Not self indulging but self fueling.

Lesson

- In what ways do you steal from your 'self' time?

- In what ways are you personally compromised when you steal from your 'self' time? i.e. not as effective, more negative, self indulging.

- What are the top 3-5 things that you NEED to do daily to really take care of yourself to be the best version of yourself so that you can be all that you want to be?

- How committed are you to your list? Is this a high enough commitment to bring the level of results you're after?

- What support can you orchestrate in advance to ensure you reach your commitment? This could be a buddy system where you encourage each other, a mentor to guide you, a coach to help you dig deep to uncover your motivation and stretch you.

Chapter 8—With Three, The Weave Is Tight

H ave you ever played, *who had the worst day* game? Someone tells you about some negative, awful thing, which happened to them, and then someone else says, "You think that's bad, let me tell you what happened to me!" And on it goes, with the ending result being a winner, who expects to receive pity for their "worst" day, and a loser who thinks that their scenario should have won, but got voted down, and giving the prize of *pity* to the winner is not their priority, because they are still stuck on a *me focus*. I have discovered, by witnessing and participating in this game myself, that it is a very unproductive activity, and often self-destructive.

From 1987 through 1988, I was a sales manager at the same company my husband worked for, but in a different division. It was at this time that I had my first experience in playing the *who had the worst day* game. The goal of the game was to have my own husband feel sympathetic towards me because of the really tough day I had, and that I should receive extra recognition for 'all that I did' and 'working so hard,' under very adverse conditions.

The problem was, that I never felt really good, or cleansed, or encouraged, or more loved, or more anything, positive. I realized that it was my inner desire for recognition that was driving me to this negative, destructive behavior, and which was actually having an unraveling effect on the *unity-weave* in our marriage—the exact opposite of tightening our marriage bond, which is what I was trying to seek.

For me it was the dawning realization that I must go back to big picture, and the desire for unity and a strong weave.

What I learned was this: when I eliminate the personal bumps in the road as being my focus for the day, and instead invite the *glue of gratefulness* in, by looking for "3's" in my day, a whole new dynamic takes place.

The 3's are:

> *What did I do, see, or experience today that spoke to me about "us."*
>
> *What did I see, hear, or experience you doing that reminds me of your love, your kindness, and your caring self.*
>
> *With this daily ritual, there is an ooze of glue that seals tightly the bond that we have.*

A complete thinking shift is required by me to not *hang on* to what happened *to me*, or what I refer to as a *clenched-fist stance*. Instead, I work towards an *open, giving, hand stance,* which allows giving and receiving.

For me, to go from a search for sympathy and recognition, to a search for gratefulness and gratitude, required me to drink a major truth serum. I had to be honest with myself—honest about my actions that were destructive. Sharing with my husband how I thought or felt I had been *wronged* that day, or pointing out to him my admiration for what someone else's husband had accomplished, or bought, was not only destructive but self-defeating, for both of us. I had to realize that in unloading and unburdening myself, I really sowing the seeds of un-appreciation and disrespect for the current effort my husband was putting forth, and it reeked of selfishness.

I had to go back to what my purpose in marriage was. If it was unity, why was I chipping away at that every day by playing the sympathy game? I had to take responsibility for my words and honestly consider *is what I'm going to say, kind or selfish*? Am I really searching for three burdens that I have re-worked mentally all day long, in order to receive the reward of sympathy, and then go on to display or act out feelings of hurt, anger, or resentment, when my husband did not give me enough *credit* for the suffering I had been through?

I prayerfully looked to the Lord for a major *help,* because I know that His love surpasses all human frailty and failings. His love fills me with what I need every day and allows *Grace* to work in me and through me. With a softened heart, the glue of gratitude can flow again, and the weave is strengthened with a daily tightening and nurturing through this new method of fortifying the marriage bond.

Lesson

- Stop right now, and take out a piece of paper, or write in the space on this page, three things you are grateful for about your husband today . . . now!

- From that list what one thing are you most grateful for and can call him right now and share with him?

- Call NOW!

Can you feel that flow begin?

Chapter 9—Giving More Of What You Want

Growing up as a middle child, and being ten years old, I quickly learned that being noticed usually came from doing something *unacceptable*, or something *over the top*. *Unacceptable* was not a path I wanted to travel, because in it I saw the rejection, isolation and hurt my brothers and sisters had gone through when they had received poor grades, or had not done their chores, or had stayed out too late. I was just hoping to be noticed for the good things I did, such as taking extra time in making the kitchen shine before going to bed. I can remember, at ten years-old taking apart the stove top in order to clean every groove and crevice, thinking that for sure my mom would notice the difference and give me a hug, a smile, or a *wow* the next morning. And I was always devastated the next morning to hear my mother go on and on about what a beautiful job my sister had done. And when I tried to tell her that I was the one who had cleaned it, she smiled and said, that *was nice of you to help*.

I was crushed—too young to be taken seriously. I took this to mean that I must do more to earn attention and praise. Whatever I did, I had to do it when I could be seen as the doer, and I had to do it often enough to increase the odds of being noticed.

As you may imagine, I practically outdid myself as I planned my *doings* in such a way that it would be noticeable and I would be recognized.

It was in my reading of *Keep A Quiet Heart*, by Elizabeth Elliot, that I was struck with the insight that God sees all that I do, no matter what, and that my purpose should be to honor

HIM first in all that I do, and to live my life for the purpose of being honorable to HIS purposes, not mine. What that meant to me was that I had to learn to let go of my focus on how much recognition *I* would receive, and instead begin to look at whether *He* would be pleased. In whatever I accomplished, would I hear from Him, "*Well done, good and faithful servant? Hmmmm.*

I then began a serious examination of my motives. *Was I serving, or was I doing just to be noticed*? A painful exploration of my soul was next. What I honestly unearthed, deep in my heart, was that much of my doing, was for recognition, and the hope of hearing, "*Great job,*" or "*Thank you,*" or "*I can't believe how hard you worked, or how much you went out of your way*". This was a painful truth serum but ultimately helpful, as it allowed me to open up and to receive further training on being *servant-hearted*. The mining, coupled with guidance from my life coach and mentor, Joe, resulted in giving me *more* of what I wanted, and helped me to begin living with being focused on Christ's purpose for my life. Finally, I was able to experience a true servant's heart and the enjoyment of genuine giving, and the serendipity of receiving back more of what I gave.

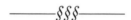

What is the one thing that you would like more of? Are you able to go to a place where you can see yourself genuinely giving, and then be able to experience that complete feeling? Can you see and feel that as being different from *giving to receive*? What are the details of your experience? Make a note right now, so you can reflect on that moment when you are looking to go back to that place.

Stopping to ask yourself, *why am I doing what I'm doing, and who am I serving by doing,* gives you a noticeable shift in perspective. It also opens thoughts to questions such as, "Could you please?" instead of "I need," or "Is it possible?" instead of "Where are you going?" These are examples of noticeable language shifts which bring amazing results in getting more of what you are giving at that moment, and the result is so much more . . . kindness.

Lesson

- Make a list of 10 things you would like more of . . .

    1 . . .

    2 . . .

    3 . . .

    4 . . .

    5 . . .

    6 . . .

    7 . . .

    8 . . .

    9 . . .

    10 . . .

- What is one thing from this list that *you* could give *your spouse* TODAY?

- Describe what that would look like.

- Would you be willing to do this, TODAY??

I would love to have you share with me your experience of doing this TODAY for your spouse at charlottevolsch@me.com.

Chapter 10—Being "Queen" Has Responsibility: *Not Just Being Served, But Elevated To Serve Many*

I n 1997, I was watching the beautiful parade of Queen Elizabeth II of England on television and noticed almost reverence in the air. With due respect, all were standing or bowing in her presence as she went by, elevated on a throne, with her crown in place.

It was a beautiful sight to be sure, but I sensed an emptiness to the scene. There was respect and honor coming from a great many people, but I did not detect a mood of gratefulness from the crowd.

I was reflecting on this when I considered the term Q*ueen of the House*. My feeling was that I would want to *earn* that position of honor and respect because of what I contributed, not because of who I am.

Twenty-four years into my marriage, I have had the privilege of experiencing true honor, love, and respect from my amazing husband.

In 2007, after noticing an enlargement in my groin, I was later diagnosed with having a *sebaceous cyst,* which needed to be removed immediately because it had grown twice as large as its detected size within two months. With my independent thinking of, *I can take care of myself,* I was totally knocked to my knees when I later developed an extreme reaction to the post-surgery mega doses of antibiotics. It was a humbling experience.

I had *reactive arthritis,* where my knees swelled to the size of grapefruit, and I literally could not stand and walk without help. What a *wow* moment for me—no more, *I am woman, hear me roar*!

The pain in my knees was excruciating, and mind-consuming. It was so loud in my mind that it was difficult to think of anything, or anyone else. I could only sleep in hour-long stretches and would drift in and out of slumber. I would restlessly try to find a comfortable position for my legs that would stop the pains from shooting like lightning bolts through my knees. With this all-consuming side affect, care for the incision from the cyst removal became totally unimportant to me.

My doctor was seriously concerned about infection and for doing an additional surgery, without a daily cleansing and dressing of my incision. She volunteered to do the cleansing and dressing, but because her office was quite a distance from my home, she suggested that a visiting nurse come by daily. I called the visiting nurse company that she suggested, and for two weeks someone came to my home to gently but thoroughly clean my incision, and to dress it once a day. The nurse would kindly talk to me, constantly checking to make sure she was not hurting me, as I winced and wiggled to find comfort for my legs in the awkward position she had to work in. I tried to convince her through clenched teeth that she was not hurting me, but the pain that I was feeling was in a totally different part of my body—my knees.

After the two-week contract was up, Cecil asked the nurse to teach him how to do the cleansing and the dressing. He felt confident he would be able to follow the steps completely and this would ensure a twice a day changing, which my doctor said would speed up the healing time, and she was uncomfortable with Cecil doing the procedure because he was my husband. I told her I was very blessed to have a husband who loved me deeply and wanted to take care of me.

I felt so loved and very humbled by this tender daily care. I was truly his queen. He was down on his knees everyday, twice each day, cleansing and redressing my incision, helping me struggle to the restroom, one tiny hesitant step at a time, cooking me something to eat, or whipping up a protein smoothie, as the nausea I had from the pain medication violently wrenched my whole body. I was losing weight without having any extra weight to lose.

Cecil's care did not extend to me only, but to Conrad as well, in checking his homework and taking him to his activities, which included karate.

It opened my eyes to what selfless serving was all about—giving without an expected return, giving out of nothing but total love. I cannot recall another time in my life when I had so powerfully felt such serving love—a true Christ-like love. It created a place for me to go back to in my mind, when I needed a refresher on what it meant to be servant-minded.

To reach my servant's heart requires prayer time every day in my morning ritual of reading, writing, praying, and exercise. I seek God's help to open my eyes to my husband and to those God places in my path for care. I pray for my heart to be humbled as I serve. When I purposefully reconnect with Him throughout the day, it gives me a wake up, a jolt, to get back on track and to reconnect with His purpose of serving. Because of these daily, purposeful rituals and steps I am moved to serve my husband out of love, and not out of duty.

I gladly do his laundry and fold it into the nice, neat stacks that he likes. I precisely prepare his breakfast with multiple spices cooked into his vegetable egg dish. I thoughtfully ask questions about his day to gently remind him of things he has committed to do, and to help offload some things that others on our business team could handle, to give his day more of a smooth flow.

The requirement to fulfill this role of a humble servant's heart and a quiet spirit is only achieved with Christ constantly by my side. This refocuses me on serving, as opposed to *what am I going to get* today.

My *daily thanksgiving log* in the evenings brings me back full circle from my morning ritual, to a place of gratitude that is focused on my husband. I look for three things that I am grateful for, that he might have done, or that he represented by his actions, or which came from who he was. I have the ritual programmed into my calendar, as I do with all of my important appointments. It does not matter that I might feel like poking his eyes out from something he said or did that day. I sit and reflect on what one thing I am grateful for, which allows my thoughts to thaw out. It allows a small crack for the light to break through, of grace and forgiveness, which leads to some other point that I am grateful for. This also benefits going to sleep at each night with good thoughts on my mind.

<u>Lesson</u>

- For the next week, my suggestion to you is that you decide upon a time of day that works best for you, either morning, afternoon or evening, and then come up with some type of alarm or trigger, to remind you of the time.

- Entering it into your electronic calendar as a scheduled activity, along with all the other things you are doing to be successful in your home and business, may work best

- Another way is to set up page in your notepad, journal, *Ever Note,* or other electronic notebook, where you can assign daily thanksgiving entries, and add to it, daily. Have a list at the top to help jog your thoughts and memory: *how he is, who he is, what he does, what he said.*

- I challenge you to fold this ritual into your day for the next week. Push past any critical spirit that comes up, or any *I want to poke his eyes out* thoughts that might surface. Then, check back with me at *charlottevolsch@me.com* and let me know if this spiritual discipline has allowed you to change the thoughts or feelings you were having daily throughout the week.

Chapter 11—Having Strength Requires A Workout Ritual— Not at the Gym . . . With HIM!

I love working out and feeling stronger, day by day. I love the control I have over my morning ritual. M aking it the important thing in tracking my day begins by preparing for it the night before. I plan my mornings in my *cubby space,* which is a small closet-type room. I set out what I will read, my journal book that I will write in, the praise music or inspirational message I will listen to, and my water and vitamins with which to start my day before my physical workout.

It was not always this way for me. In fact, I was of the mindset that my true strength came from myself. I thought that I had to work hard to make it a growing reality, by studying, practicing, and learning from others who had already done what I was trying to do. Don't get me wrong: those are all important steps, but until I learned where the true strength came from, the inner strength, the operating strength, I was wearing myself out.

It was easy to get caught up in life and to let God sit on the back burner until a need would arise. Not until a crisis broke out did I consider going to my knees with my *wish list* for a resolution to the crisis at hand. My *wish list* included the steps I thought necessary to resolve the conflict, and with the magical speediness of God's help, I believed it could work out, if He was listening. Wow, how prideful of me to think that God was my *genie in a bottle,* so to speak!

So how was I able to make the transition?

In 2,000, I began a new awakening and a new journey with Christ. Although I was raised in a Christian home I never learned about having a personal relationship with Christ. Looking back, it makes me smile to think how treated my connection with God as if He was a genie—something to turn off and on at will. In March, 2000, I was introduced to having a relationship with Christ through the eyes of his Mother Mary in a pre-Easter program my friend Yvette had taken me to. As the mother of a three year-old, I was touched to the depth of my soul with Mary's joy, as well as her anguish in raising Jesus, watching Him teach many, and then be brutally tortured and killed before her eyes. It ripped my heart out to feel her pain, and it awakened me to the reality of having a personal relationship with Him.

A relationship required development and that development would require much on my part. I would need to commit to, and be willing to invest daily, in working on this relationship, to the same degree that I was working on my relationship in being a mom to my son.

Wow, that was a lot of time to invest, I thought, but I so wanted what Yvette already had, especially her sense of peace and calmness during life's storms, a sense of what to do next.

When her five year-old daughter had an appendicitis attack, I watched her gather her things together, to leave for the hospital, with a peaceful aura about her. It was the same type of peacefulness that I had felt from seeing Christ's mother, Mary, in the play, and it made that connection so much more human for me. I had to transform my belief in what I saw into action steps that could bring me to that peaceful relationship. I was willing to humble myself and ask: *what next do I need to learn or do?*

How do I give grace?

How can I be gracious?

How can I flush out my critical spirit?

How can I be kind when I'm hurting myself?

How can I forgive when I feel violated?

I learned daily and throughout each day to make time to go to Him in conversation, prayer, and praise, even if my only *alone time* was in the bathroom. I learned about studying and reading the Word, to gain additional insights, and to hear Him speak to me, not w i t h a lightning bolt of revelation, but r a t h e r , w i t h an *ah ha* moment, of *now I understand a little bit more.* I would go to Him many mornings, with tears streaming down my cheeks, as I ran on the treadmill during my morning workout hour, asking for help to see the path I was to s u p p o s e d be on, asking for His help to have the right words to communicate encouragement to my husband as he was learning a new industry. I would cry out to Him, to awaken my husband to what he needed to be working on, too.

Day after day I would read, run, pour my heart out, pull on my armor and prepare for a new day. The impact of me not bringing in income for the t h i r d year was taking its toll on all of us, and combined with Cecil's sales territory being cut back dramatically, it gave me an awakening to God's p r o m p t i n g t h a t w e n e e d e d to m a k e a complete career shift.

The daily process of digging deep within myself, to see what hurt or resentment I needed to flush out a n d replace with encouragement, and kindness, and love, was often draining; and yet it was very encouraging as well. I could truly feel the flow of His strength in this new relationship—giving me focus and direction, a path to run on, and a *realness* to my sense of direction.

Cecil and I had begun reading together daily from "The Bible In One Year" series, which b r o u g h t me new insights, not only f r o m the readings, but also on God's heart, and a fresh commitment to grow in my walk with Him.

In 2007, I was introduced to the concept of a consistent morning ritual by my coach, Joe Stumpf, which resonated within me to make this time f i l l e d w i t h meaning and purpose. This allowed me to start my day effectively, as I continued to grow i n my walk, and to deepen my relationship with Christ.

In 2009, my friend, Gaye, suggested to me a book that her women's ministry group was reading at church. She told me that she had an extra copy to share with me.

"Gaye, that sounds so great! How about we read it together and share with each other weekly what we learn from each chapter?"

So began a prayer partner/reading partner relationship, which helped immensely and continues to help me stay strong in life's battles. It has often been the nudge to think past *me,* to the bigger picture. Gaye and I have been faithful in that relationship for over fourteen years, and through our weekly readings of fifteen different books, we have encouraged each other through victories, losses, hurts, trials, and joys.

Like a physical workout, where the body grows stronger, the spiritual workout brings more inner peace, calmness, and joy, because of a daily connectedness—almost like recharging a battery. The commitment to continually work on *myself*—not my husband, not my child, nor anyone else in my world but just me, is astounding. I look back now, thirteen years later, and do not even recognize the *me* of 2,000.

Like my physical self, I never do get to a place called *done.* With a daily focus and committed effort, I do not look for *done,* anymore; I look for *better*!

Lesson

- In your daily life, do you see a place where you can go for you time, with Christ relationship building as a goal?

- What can you see in your life that you could bring to that place, daily? i.e. Bible, journal, a headset for listening quietly to praise music, or an inspiring message.

- At what time in your day could you use, to make that time a special ritual? Early before your house rises? In the evening, or afternoon, when nobody else is around?

- Who in your life could you invite in as an accountability partner, to encourage you, and to be encouraged?

- Let me know how I can help with your next step.

Chapter 12—Soft Strength, Strong Success

I n 1998, after twenty years of solid, committed investment and loyalty to a fortune 250 company, the rules suddenly changed affecting our retirement plan.

Earnings during retirement would be cut by 50% from the original package for Cecil, because he missed being *grandfathered* in from the original plan by one year.

I had lived through seventeen of those twenty years and had witnessed the hours of training he had put in, as well as the coaching and training he had done for others. Here, at the start of a new chapter in his life, as a dad and family man, employment stability was becoming more and more elusive. Fear of what was coming next and resentment against the company for placing so little value on "all those years of dedication and loyalty," combined with my leaving the work force and having our income drop by fifty percent, was a fearful thought.

My prayer for my husband was for him to realize his bigger potential, now that the opportunity was open for him to embark upon a new career direction. Much encouragement and reinforcement was going to be required to make the transition, and for him to become a success.

My prayer for myself was to be filled with words of encouragement and strength, as my husband would now be taking on two jobs: the one he knew, and an apprenticeship in the one he was learning.

Twelve years later, in a room filled with hundreds of people ready to learn and to take notes, it was my husband's turn to take the stage and to share with everyone his tools for success.

He scanned the group and began with an amazingly well-planned, and effective, teaching session. As I looked out over the sea of faces, I could tell that his presentation was being well-received. But I knew that the only face that really mattered to Cecil was the one that had been there, encouraging him, and reviewing his rough draft over the past weeks. It was the face with my smile that I knew would matter most.

For me, putting aside my personal needs, my disappointments, my frustrations, my *me-me-me* thoughts, was a bitter pill to swallow, but it was necessary in order to allow the spirit within me to flow out. To allow my encouraging *self*, my *I'm proud of you* self, my *thinking past me self*, to see the greatness in Him.

I love the peacefulness that comes over me when I allow this *me that I love being*, to surface. The spirit of being an encourager now comes very natural to me. I constantly look for filling the entire glass. But when I think about what could have been—had I dismissed *encourager* and invited in the *judger*—I can only imagine the results! With *judger* I would have regressed backwards, damaged my inner spirit (as well as my husband's), and added another more layers of resentment and disgust to my inner core.

It was only through my willingness to admit to myself my weaknesses, and to go in prayer to seek Christ's forgiveness and strength, that I can now invite HIM to open that rusted gate of grace, and to allow another's humanity to shine, even with all the scales and scars, and to glow with greatness, kindness, and possibilities.

As I pulled into the park on the corner of Rancho Road and Margarita Parkway, I sat for a minute taking in the beauty of the golden trees and to watch the ducks scurrying about on the grassy bank. I could feel a smile breaking across my face as I listened to their honks while they scuffled about.

I got out of my car and slowly strolled over to the park bench on the opposite bank of the pond, which allowed me the ability to observe their hectic feasting on the scattered bread without having to listen to the high volume of their quacking. As I looked out across the pond, I noticed a sole swan gliding across the water. There was barely a disturbance to the still water as she gracefully swam in a way that seemed effortless! I quietly stayed where I was and inched my way to the edge of the pond, first standing still, then squatting, so as not to disturb her motion or to startle her. The water appeared very smooth from this perspective and gave me a clear picture of what was going on below the water—a flurry of paddling, like a small paddle boat! Yet, above the water, remained the peaceful, quiet, seemingly effortless gliding.

There was a time that I was much like those ducks. I was self-absorbed. I was flapping and clacking for recognition, like those ducks on the grass. I was honking to bring attention to the fact that I was *right* this time. I was waddling about with a suitcase full of *all I had done*. I was wallowing in the self-satisfaction of being the *winner* of the day, or of the argument, or of the discussion.

I can see now, how I have progressed in becoming like the swan. I am working intentionally on myself below the water through daily rituals. I am building grooves through these patterns, and in my home. I have shed my *coat of competitive spirit;* I have unbuttoned my *sweater of recognition;* I have removed my *scarf of winner*. I now search for what is right in my husband. I work at choosing words to encourage more of what he wants. I now look at the world more from the perspective of *Us*.

Like the swan who does not see herself as smooth and graceful gliding effortlessly across the water, I have been told that my relationship with my husband appears to have been built without effort. The reality, however, is the work that I began years ago has never stopped, and continues daily with work and practice. I pay attention. I choose wisely to be the wife that my husband needs. My fight against selfishness is a daily commitment that I have chosen to make.

I hate the responsibility of being the *thermostat* in my home, because with it comes the reality of the results—arghh! But that is what I signed up for as a wife, and now, a mother. That is a responsibility that I know will not produce good results without the morning time I require, with God to set the tone to set me back on a firm foundation, to recalibrate myself for following His purpose for my life, and all that requires. Having a comfortable temperature in my home requires me to have a comfortable temperature within myself, and that means forgoing *what's in it for me*, *what about me*, and *who's going to help me*. Instead, it means turning to *what about you, what am I doing for you*. Finally it means, tuning in to HIS still small voice, and feeling the power of HIS soft but firm touch of support.

Lesson

- What three scenarios in life bring out the *duck* in you?

- Pick one scenario and write out what you would need to think differently, do differently and be differently to stop the *quacking and waddling* in that situation.

- Now look at that same scenario again and write out what about the scene caused you to become a *duck*.

Chapter 13—Feeling Complete

I stood looking in the mirror, in preparation for the day. Makeup on—check! I just loved the bright, bright green of the sweater, and the unusual die of the jeans that came out in green and black swirls, but yikes! Something was missing. Thank goodness I had looked in the mirror. I had forgotten to put on lipstick! Now I looked complete.

This is part of the daily survey I have to make, as I look at my daily preparation of the *total me*. Do I have my *Jesus* on! I can feel good from my physical workout; I can feel inspired from my inspirational listening; I can feel purposeful from my mailing; but I am only complete with the time I spend with HIM, reflecting on HIS purpose for my life, seeking HIS guidance in my day, and calling upon HIS forgiving spirit and grace to infuse love into my actions.

Ah, now I feel complete! And just as if I were stopping to notice in a mirror throughout the day that my lipstick needs to be reapplied, I now stop to see if HIS peaceful glow is coming through my demeanor, and whether words of kindness and encouragement are coming out of me, instead of impatience and criticism.

I want HIM with me, because having Him with me throughout the day is like having a long fleecy robe to put on when facing a chilly morning, and having HIM wrapped within me makes me feel cozy, complete, and prepared for any chill of the day.

I am past feeling inferior; I am complete in HIS love and strength. I am past feeling guilt; I am complete in HIS forgiveness.

I have surrendered and want to go where ever He points and leads me.

I am not fearful in that surrendered state, because I am so completely covered in HIS cloak of armor, which I know will protect me, no matter what.

Gone is *judgment*. Gone is *criticism*.

Welcome the *cloak of peace and protection* that transcends everything.

Feeling close to HIM is the fundamental purpose of my life. He wants ALL of me.

Without giving myself back to HIM, emptiness soon begins, and from that place the futility of searching begins.

Closeness with HIM, true closeness, is as challenging to describe, as the flood of feelings of giving birth and being a parent, to someone who is not. It can only be fully understood by someone who has experienced it themselves.

Start your own walk by demonstrating through your daily actions the reality of HIS presence, which shines forth in being *peace-centered,* and allow others to share their life perspectives with you without being judged, but at the same time with you being a guide for them to lead them to the Truth.

Lesson

- Make a list of five things you do daily or weekly for your husband.

- Now mark next to each one on a scale of 1 low, 10 high, how enthusiastically are doing each of the five things for your husband?

- Now take the one out of the five that you enjoy the least and write it out in this format: "Today I will _____ for you Lord, focusing on each step to ensure it pleases you as I reflect your light and be your hands. As I think of how I honor you by doing _____ it makes me smile NOW!"

Chapter 14—Maintaining Harmony: *In Your Christ-Centered Home*

M aintaining harmony in your Christ centered home is a daily, and day by day, journey.

If you're committed to the results and would like insights to your best next step, call 760-912-8905 or email *charlotte@volschteam.com*.

I am humbled to share with you an out-of-the-blue letter that I received earlier this year, which echoed harmony and love.

> *Dear Charlotte,*
>
> *As I think of all the circumstances that had to align across all the thousands of miles and dozens of years for our meeting, I'm convinced that it was orchestrated by God. I'm eternally grateful that we met and eventually began a new life together.*
>
> *As I reflect on all the very thin threads of circumstance that guided our meeting and the early times after we met, I'm so grateful that it happened.*
>
> *I'm grateful you had patience with me as I learned to love you, and you to love me.*

I'm grateful for the life we experienced together and the struggles we worked through in the corporate life and that we decided that we needed to leave that life.

I'm grateful that after that decision God blessed us with a great gift of parenthood, and I'm grateful you have blossomed so beautifully as a nurturing and caring mother to our son.

I'm grateful for the love you have extended to me, even when I am sometimes very hard to love.

I am grateful for you and look forward to spending the rest of my life growing closer to you as we prepare to pass the baton.

Love, Cecil

18743922R00046

Made in the USA
San Bernardino, CA
27 January 2015